Made in the USA
Coppell, TX
19 February 2022

73815938R00063